EXILE ON BEACH STREET

Exile
On Beach Street

Kevin Opstedal

San Francisco, California

© 2025 Kevin Opstedal

All rights reserved

ISBN 979-8-9921594-2-4

Some of the poems in this book first appeared (sometimes in different form) in the chapbooks, *Custom Shapes* (Repo Press, 2018), *Torching the Pier* (Blazing Stadium Pamphlet Series, 2020), *Ace of Tentacles* (Auguste Press, 2020), *Dharma Pharmacy & Surf Shop* (Bird & Beckett, 2024), the anthology *Beat Not Beat*, (Moon Tide Press, 2022), and in the following print periodicals and online journals: *Positive Magnets*, *High Noon*, *San Diego Reader*, *Poetry London*, *The Doris*, *Blazing Stadium*, *Soul Glue*, *Live Mag!*, *Castle Grayskull*, *Luigi Ten Co*, and *NEW: A Journal of American Poetry*.

Cover artwork by Pamela Dewey

Author photo by Pamela Dewey

San Francisco, California

These poems are an IOU to
Joanne Kyger, Lewis MacAdams,
Ed Dorn, Jim Carroll, & Bill Berkson

CONTENTS

I'll Have a Negra Modelo & Bring the Octopus a White Russian	1
Pump Up the Valium	2
Let's Get Lost	4
Calculating the Drift	5
Shiva's Little Grind	6
Pre-Existing Conditions	7
Sneaking a Drink w/the Tiki Blonde	8
From Malibu to Eternity	9
Enter the Tune	10
Confessing My Tattoo	11
Like Driving to Chinatown for Tacos	12
The Calypso of Eucalyptus	14
Small Fortune	15
Romance with Opiates (A Limited Engagement)	16
Odysseus Among the Lotus-Eaters	18
The Beast from 20,000 Fathoms	20
There is a Door	21
Under the Influence	22
Down in the Groove	23
A Willing Suspension of Disbelief w/a Single-Coil Pickup	24
Francis X. Bushman Rides a Boogie Board to India	25
Half-Past Guillaume Apollinaire, Pontiac Blues, & the Taco Stand on Pier Street	26
Tapping the Source	28
Anyone's Permutations Anymore Than My Own	29
Never One to Drop the Dime	31
Fake Blonde in Red	32
They Call Me Pagliacci but My Real Name is Mr. Earle	33
The Phone is Ringing	34
Casual Mythology	35
Conspiring to Hijack My Otherwise Delicate Sensibilities	37
Lifted From the Proverbs	38

Revealing a Formal Existence Independent of the Russet Sky	39
Long Past Gone	40
Loading History	41
Ace of Tentacles	42
The Name of the Rose	43
The Thomas de Quincey Shuffle	44
Devotions (after Rimbaud)	45
At Bolinas	46
Suzie Q Does the Zombie Twist	47
If I Wrote This in Tijuana 40 Years Ago Would I Remember?	48
Mr. Zog's 3-Day Nocturne	49
Black Ops	50
Bach's Toccata & Fugue in D Minor vs The Belairs Mr. Moto	51
The Scene of the Crime	52
Let There Be Lithium	53
The Last Car That Parked Here is Still Missing	54
Next Time I'll Build You a Mai Tai	55
Manchurian Space Reggae	56
Conflict Resolution Among the Mouth Breathers	57
Dancing to Elevator Music in the Stairwell	58
Finding the Lost Chord on a Plastic Souvenir Ukulele	59
A Guide to Self-Medication	60
You'd Better Have a Plan B	61
Second-Hand Smokescreen	62
Where Have All the Payphones Gone	63
Revving It Up Between Su Tung-p'o & the Notebooks of Shelley	64
Skimming the Surface	65
Drop C Tuning for Steam-Driven Guitar	67
Pier Pressure	71
I Thought to Roll Up My Sleeves but the Light Had Been Encrypted & My Tattoo Didn't Translate	72
Roll Bounce	73

40 Ounce Blues	74
Torch Ballad w/a Menthol Filter	76
I Hear a Symphony	77
Shine a Light	78
Painting Shadows	79
From a Motel Room in Venice	80
Dropping in on a Floater	81
Bending Like a Spoon to the Flame	82
Exile on Beach Street	84
Hong Kong Blues	85
Walking Tiptoe Thru the Ruins of Western Civilization (w/Headphones On)	86
Tijuana Gift Shop	87
Alien vs Predator, or The Last Days of Disco	89
A Twofer at the Five & Dime	90
Riding a Piano into the Unknown	91
Riffle Shuffle	92
Sliding Down the Ladder of a True Believer Before the Light Changes	93
Mixing Up the Medicine	96
Subliminal Cutback	97
The Zen of Wearing Sunglasses at the Movies	98
A Different Dynamic	99
Playing the Percentages	100
They Call the Wind (Cholita)	101
The Smog's Vibrant Gown	102
Lowering the Boom	103
Going the Distance	104
What's Your Metaphor?	105
Nice Catch	106
3,000 Crooked Miles to Honolulu	107
Roll Me a Pearl	108
The Obliteration of the Self as Evidenced in Wittgenstein's Surf Almanac	111
Surfing by Candlelight	112
An Ounce of Nightingale vs Banjos in the Eucalyptus	113

Retracing the Steps of a Last Tango & My Hesitation to Bail on the Scene	114
Carmen & the Devil Ride a Mule Thru a Field of Poppies	116
Wearing Yesterday Like Tomorrow	117
Tea for Two Minus One & Counting	118
Stalling for Depth	120
Show Me the Way to Go Home	122
The Spanish Prisoner	123

I'LL HAVE A NEGRA MODELO
& BRING THE OCTOPUS A WHITE RUSSIAN

The way that story ended is
how this one begins
                                      another missed shot
                 falling short of the paradox
w/a little R&R between nosebleeds
         that we might learn to distinguish the
                              murmur of eucalyptus leaves
from the blue lemon sky
                     in a zip-lock bag

        The ocean-colored ocean
                & a heavy slab of sunset

            Loaves & fishes   Stems & seeds

    snap decisions broken in half
        by a misjudged floater
                on the wrong side of the jetty

I never planned on being here this long
        never read the small print
                never heard the warning bell at lights out
                        echoing long before it struck

How often like a thief
sleepwalking from Tehuantepec to Kubla Khan
loaded to the springs

PUMP UP THE VALIUM

Shorter Days Longer Sleeves
Not light, not dark, but in between
& proprietary
    just as one thing
        leads the other into the next
walking in circles on Front Street near the beach
under the Slowtember sky
    bleached-blonde vato language
        & a sea-breeze to hear it through
on cither side of yr wanting something
        whatever the reason
as I see you now
        leaning into the mist
w/yr eyes all lit up
    like an Ensenada drug store

Bo Diddley's Beach Party
Versus the relentless chiaroscuro I've got a flashlight
    & a lifetime subscription to
        the sky over Hermosa Beach

Versus the wild pink yonder I've got a full-scale replica of the
    Pyramid of the Sun at Teotihuacàn
        hand-painted on the waves

Versus an avalanche of diesel-powered harmonicas
    I've got a minute of silence
        wearing infinite space like a cement kimono

Versus you just sitting there
    waiting for me to say the wrong thing
        I've got 36 chainsmoking buddhas
            preaching the kind of punk compassion
                we could really dance to

Plastic Flamingo
Aside from the fact
                    or because of it
the light falling
            against the water or the
sand or pavement I thought was
                    our self-fulfilled prophecy
the virtue inherent in any vice
            stumbling like a tear
& the calculated risk her silk & lace describe against the
smooth continuum her skin insists upon
                    to be random & precise
unaffected by exposure even
    as those reclusive inventories
                        in the hollows
            parallel to bent strands of pearl indulgence
snap back into the standard pulsing rhythm none of us understand
or really listen to anymore

& down the street from there
            her shadow falls like a hammer
    but the flickering celluloid sky
                        ain't feeling it

LET'S GET LOST

I decided that yr eyes are like
the pigeons of the Holy Ghost
roosting upon the Temple of Ephesus at dawn
or was it the Ventura pier at sunset?

Either way the rustling of wings
took me back to the
                    palm trees of Venice
              & the Egyptian labyrinth of
                    alleyways I trekked every
                            day on my way to the beach

It never ends until it does like breathing
& to cross the furious tropic of dreams
learning to talk in the kind of broken
English that could fill a book of haikus
only confirms love's tiptoe approach

but the heart's a slow train
dragging thru quicksand
          a book of soggy matches vs Godzilla
                rocks that blink when stared at
        the moan of a rusty harmonica
                        bending palm trees in the fog

Side effects may include
invincibility, a trick knee, the Hully Gully,
& a feeling for leaving

CALCULATING THE DRIFT

A drive up the coast
behind the wheel of an awkward silence
doesn't allow for the
heavy ordinance

nor the charming way the woman
        beside you bites her lips when
                you speed-shift around those blind curves
                      singing off-key

The doctor says it's
bad for my thermostat
but I say it isn't the song so much as
how you sing it

        Pomp & circumstantial evidence
            racing past the
                    Department of Planned Obsolescence

& less than a mile from there it
all turns to glass
            which shatters when you
hit the high notes

SHIVA'S LITTLE GRIND

Silver-green eucalyptus leaves
shimmering in the wind
like a school of sardines in the shallows

        Another day it might be like the way it felt to
        read *Confessions of an English Opium Eater*
        in 1822
                the fog rolling in from the beach
the sun a disk of tarnished
silver nailed to the sky

        & maybe she walks in beneath it
            as I reach out to her
                with two or more hands

Her eyes like dark stretches of intertidal static
raking the dust of Darwinian succession
in blue suede huaraches

PRE-EXISTING CONDITIONS

Love's Apparition & Evanishment
I thought it was seawater
      dripping into my ear
  but it was only the ocean fog
        tapping at the window

Torquing the Lyric Vibe
Splash of sunrise deep
   purple into razor-pink
      robbing the shadow of a liquor store
w/a squirt gun
       & you were there
         pretending you weren't
   as the hinges fell off the
        door to my heart

A Date w/Gravity
Sometimes you're like a balcony I can leap from
other times you're like a glass of water I'm
diving into
from an impossible height

SNEAKING A DRINK W/THE TIKI BLONDE

I haven't forgotten
           even if I can't remember

the root connection
dealt out in small doses at Lulu's
Bait & Switch Shop

        just another way to
                blunt the needle

an elbow of sand bumping up against a
shoulder of concrete
      beneath a throwdown neon sunset
          planted in leaning whispers
                that fill cracks in the seawall

as it would be a
                reckoning of sorts
requiring the application of counterweights
      along w/enough saltwater kool-
          aid to strip the paint from
the walls of yr soul

or at least enough to
skim the bliss off a last tango like mist
sheering the sky from the pavement

FROM MALIBU TO ETERNITY

The concrete steps that led
down to the beach
were covered in seaweed & wet
sand the color of yr eyes
I was sipping the salt mist
you were sliding past all that
like a shadow on stained glass
I taught myself Spanish
just so I could sing along
& w/the hazy blue sky melting
like a Mars bar on the lid of yr heart
I did the Shuffle, I did the Stroll, I did the
Quasimodo

ENTER THE TUNE

Stars over Monterey Bay

The moon in a black limousine

& I'm not sure but the light could be
        sharpening itself on the edge of
                1001 dark nights of the soul

                        & now it's me
standing face to face
        w/someone that looks like
the you
        I never knew
                gazing into my eyes
w/the same blank stare that
        launched a thousand ships

CONFESSING MY TATTOO

The ocean shimmers
like a thin line of
bluegreen neon lip gloss
smeared against the sky at sunset
& I'm feeling as responsible as a Hawaiian cocktail
spilled on the sidewalk
in front of the pier
sinking beneath the weight of
pale pink angels who
talk out the side of their mouths
& carry guitars zipped up in body bags

I'd like to trade in those scrap-iron halos
for a primer gray belch-fire El Camino
then gun the engine while chasing down the
starlet who wears crooked shoes

I'm burning out the clutch
& she's got black silk eyes

LIKE DRIVING TO CHINATOWN FOR TACOS

Easy Does It
Cranking up the dial on noise
a windy day keeps the palm trees busy

the sky swarming w/something that
is usually only found in the pages of a
classical dictionary

like a dogeared surfboard
w/independent rear suspension
& eccentric punctuation
navigating the maelstroms & lulls that
get sucked down the drain

a spinning feather of pearly time

Landing on Water
It isn't far from the highway
        a steep arroyo that cuts down thru
                poison oak and coyote brush
maybe deer tracks in the soft silt sand
        nestled between rocks older than the
                water that carved them
& near the bottom
raw Pacific salt mist lifted from
        ditch marshes of slime & mud & pickleweed
w/interrogating butterflies & wrens or
        wren-like small birds
                darting among weeds
brown flash feathers & quick eyes that
        you either saw or remembered seeing
The least breeze rattling
                the rusted-out warning sign
        graffitied into obscurity
                      above a broken square of

    bleached concrete & sand
            still wet from the receding tide
dark & glistening
     like Medusa & the two-way mirror
          versus Moaning Lisa & her monkey eyes
sometimes all it takes is a speck of blue sky
     w/the ocean rushing in beneath it

Live From the Impact Zone
Anyone says the obvious
oblivious
this
that I might have otherwise answered
w/a Renaissance bump
               nuanced (due west
        & south near
              the halfway mark
            depending on yr point of view)
as we tumble towards a
tidepool rendezvous
        if only to partake in a little
              voodoo facetime
while I search for the access code
to yr heart
        & the catchy tune that it plays

THE CALYPSO OF EUCALYPTUS
for Jim Carroll

Converting iambic pentameter to
fluid ounces
folded into the legalese of
tar-streaked sand & foam
& no matter how you parse it
the luck of the draw
as much as those disciples of the Dark Rose
hooked on classics
w/jungle drums & sawed-off guitars
& every now & then the muffled
crash of waves at Topanga
relayed via the molecular theory
of an 8-track cassette tape
w/rambling bird notes
pending comprehension
if only to provoke these sordid blessings
& the voracious discontent of our
sometime resolve
falling past the lark & seagull sky
like a refrigerator
full of adrenalin

SMALL FORTUNE

Evidently a Design Flaw
I concentrated on my footwork which
she insisted on referring to as an "exit
strategy" but I wasn't so sure of the
rhyme scheme in the third stanza

24 Hours to Kill
"If you are expecting poetry to
tell you something you can use, you better
reconsider the wings on the poet's sandals
and the rules of the game Elegua plays"
— Duncan McNaughton

Desperate Measures
The distribution of the
divine graces plus seven
sacraments & the over-
whelming realization that
you can't run from a gorilla

Christ dragging his cross thru yr flesh like a plow
She had that "Let's get
hammered" look in her eyes
& I said that I would meet her
halfway there

ROMANCE WITH OPIATES (A LIMITED ENGAGEMENT)

It has to do with balance
        the inner ear listening to something else entirely
"Spare change?" (Not today)
                I was listening for once
                          (for a change)
Motors Running in the Fog
Memory's Gracious Gift
                  (thinking this)

& like threading the needle w/a sledgehammer
rusted nasturtium leaves
        ready to give up the ghost
                tremble in the late summer breeze
as the sun drops
        behind the rim of the tide
   w/bandaged wings
                & chrome-plated resolve

& so that muted sparkle as of damped chords
ringing
     & you stepping out
            in your see-thru camouflage
w/radiant wheels of sunlight
        grinding against the tempered
                steel of a relentless sky

        Now you see it / Now you don't

like a Jedi mind trick
at dark of noon beneath your midnight sunburn

For what lingers there after is no adjunct
where chopped seas in concert w/the spilled tequila
Centenario Anejo
    && yr eyes like suicide calypsos walking away
        to resume the simple rules of the bent fan blade

Several other worlds intersect or overlap this one
    each with its own catalog of greasy regrets
  & like a desperate attempt at setting the world's
        record for heavy breathing
the wind that ripples thru the cypress
        sings an octave higher in the eucalyptus

ODYSSEUS AMONG THE LOTUS-EATERS

Not a single twisted spoonful of
numb surprise
to offset the shake & bake light all
darkwater turquoise w/aloha pipes

      but out near the latitude of Tacos Locos
      beneath the relentless ocean haze

& the sunlight
bending that way in the
dark mirrors that are her eyes

      w/hints of flamingo
          mother-of-pearl
              bichloride of sunset
  plus other less obvious perhaps inventories
  no doubt explicit by omission

& from there it's a clear shot to the
      ramshackle tenements of Shangri La
         w/hula-stripes & lullabies
            schooled in logic
              & blue movies at low tide

    swept up in the thick diminuendo of mist
    where Rebel Rebel meets Louie Louie
    tying knots in your veins

& like the Ten Commandments in a gorilla suit
    knocking at the screen door
the wind serenades cypress & eucalyptus
        spent dreaming still so by their restlessness

I had to reach back into my
         archive of
                  auditory hallucinations
               to find the proper
                        tone & pitch but the
sky wasn't right for
      that kind of self-incrimination

Broken waves displace the tide
      & the sun tightens up like a fist
say whatever you want it's all true
                  even when it's not
            & there's 20 miles between you & your
      mind (a distance
                  you'll probably not cover today

THE BEAST FROM 20,000 FATHOMS

Move the window slightly left of the palm tree

rain   rain   rain   rain   rain

drizzle music

        (George Frideric Handel meets the Plastic Ono Band)

drip drip drip
splash

        Underwater acoustics
        like the gong effect in a Doppler profile

or the rippling sound of what starfish might think
between tides

THERE IS A DOOR
for Miguel Price

It had all been carefully worked out
to the smallest incremental detail
w/contingencies
but things don't always go
according to plan.

A design flaw,
something broke, there was a
hiccup in the time/space
continuum, etc.

If it all falls thru
maybe it's because there is a
secret plan?

A recipe. A scheme. A formula.
A slice of slanted sunlight falling
between the Devil & a deeper shade of blue.

Everyone needs a plan.

The last time I had a plan
I woke up in San Francisco
& someone had stolen my shoes.

UNDER THE INFLUENCE

A seagull says something
                but we don't speak seagull
    dodging elbows
               among the chosen ones
          recalling the promise of a
                gnarled pair of flip-flops
& a night heron
      at the side of the road in
            Point Reyes Station that time
on our way to a funeral

an object lesson in revolving credit

      I gave only that which I could not take

          not to mention the
              pale blue octopus
                  & the pearl-handled squirt gun

      relics of some other place & time
          no one here remembers

& I can take you there
if you want
        somewhere out near
                  Dockweiler Beach
    where we don't stop
    anymore
            but if we did you'd get that
neon freeze-out you
          love so much
      & I'd fade into the Pacific-colored
            haze that the
                  sky there wears so well

DOWN IN THE GROOVE

I'm only holding on so that I can
feel it all slip away

Pursuing several
lines of inquiry
not the least of which is
raiding the fridge

It either will or it won't
change the complexion of this
late summer sky
glimpsed thru a rail of mist

like all debts
              real & imagined
a cocktail olive
                 no bigger than the South Pacific
a flock of electric eels
                    riding in on the tide
Death's big toothy grin

The wreck of the Hesperus makes a cameo appearance here
There's really nothing in the fridge
Leaps & bounds a measured response thick as a brick

Sparrows in the cypress hedge
            conspire w/the wind to
                    distract me & it works

          Subliminal Green Waves
                        (some assembly required)

A WILLING SUSPENSION OF DISBELIEF W/A SINGLE-COIL PICKUP

Just a little something for the
B-side of
                "Betty Lou Got a New Tattoo"
    scored to a
             post-apocalyptic
                        exhaust note
& the bongo relevance
        that eventually one might even
                      learn to dance to

a goatfoot shuffle across the
        sand gravel path for example

            pursuant to & not for nothing

  leading w/the middle finger

FRANCIS X. BUSHMAN RIDES A BOOGIE BOARD TO INDIA

Plunging thru & against the drift
a definite maybe in the heart's
house when no one's home

Milarepa said there are four
ways in & one way out
but then the dead don't shimmy in the stained
glass display window
& the light is like lemonade in a can
tilted in the mist above all that copper & steel
bending in the waves

A southwest swell I knew was on its way by the
ache in my knees

& like a message scrawled in lipstick on a mirror
nobody knows what it means but everyone understands it'll
break if you drop it
which is what keeps us coming back for more

HALF-PAST GUILLAUME APOLLINAIRE, PONTIAC BLUES & THE TACO STAND ON PIER STREET

Biographia Literaria Blues
Shuffling thru blank pages
in the Jim Nod Variorum
while a surfboard sleeps
in a corner of the room

Saturday Matinee
The cosmic convergence of 10,000 seagulls
maybe two or three more than that
wheeling in a great feathered vortex

Residual Topanga Drainage
Heading north on the coast highway
a baseball bat & a machete
under the seat
(variations on a theme)

Diebenkorn Cheat Sheet
A thin red line diagonal to a
scribble of turquoise
& what could be a disemboweled Chevy
sedan bleeding rust onto the pink
stucco wall of a one-bedroom rental
just steps from the beach

Slack Tide
A sea swamp veneer
accentuates the screendoor chiaroscuro

A Fist Full of Dollars
Wishing I was in Todos Santos
reading Rimbaud & wondering how to
pay for a big plate of nopales

Kicking the Gong
palm
tree
puzzle
piece

Alternating Currents
Nikola Tesla perceived the earth as a
conductor of acoustical resonance.
But what about the ocean?
What about those high-heel huaraches?

Vapor Lock
The walls are crawling
                shadows chasing light
    the gold of gray mist
                    sporting Santeria ink
& taking a deep breath
I stand & recite the following
invocation:
    1. The Hollow Pearl
    2. A Lexicon of Homeric Dialect
    3. Ocean sunset in a trance
    4. Try Stinson Beach Surf & Kayak. Ask for Donnie.

TAPPING THE SOURCE
for Eddie Ainsworth

If Every Gateway Drug Lived Up to Its Name
A late afternoon sky
w/vinyl upholstery & tinted windows is
parked above the beach

radiance / alignment / balance

    & the tendency of a system to oscillate at a
    greater amplitude at some frequencies
    than at others

                        (which I don't understand
except for the vowel sounds

Aspect Ratio
This morning there's a moderate SW swell w/a low grade NW in
the background. Well exposed south-facing beaches are seeing sets
running chest-plus & clean, w/light wind, as the dropping tide
helps speed things up. Given the distance & a 45-degree trajectory,
the next swell looks to be just some sporadic angular-spread
energy from a system that spun off Antarctica SE of New Zealand
late last week. Its promise is like a light burning in the refrigerator
even when the door is shut.

Water on Mars
I swore I heard Sweet Jane's kid sister
calling the little red rooster
& the foam
rushing up across the sand
was like a game of Chinese whispers

ANYONE'S PERMUTATIONS ANYMORE THAN MY OWN

One After 909
The mythology of a last damp toke
riding off into the sunset
    like Lao Tzu's lost thesis on
        oceanography
                w/trembling Spanish interiors
              & a kind of rumbling indifference
                      you can feel in yr bones

The warp of road subsequent
    all dressed in black
        & walking like a Peloponnesian

            dependent upon a parallel vocabulary
                hardwired to the pavement

Bruised Knuckles
Heavy weather on the coast
    brewed in a Tahitian swamp
w/diminished returns
    crumbling even the sea wall beneath the sun
upside-down
        sketched out in blurry
                sacrificial haze

A step defines entrance even as it fades
        across that line the tide set later

    Offshore music
            leaning against the wind

A centrifugal engagement of gulls
        lulled into degrees of difficulty

A Barely Sustainable Indulgence
The rusty sludge of sunset an
emblem of the
general decay perhaps the air around
Pompeii (for example)

    & mapping the tides to China & back
    playing it by ear

        every wave wash, foam bubble, seashell—

remember the difference
            (between this one & that
  one)
      & the light . . .

          a decorative occasion
              all amethyst & neon

reduced to a blue so pale it
tastes pure white

NEVER ONE TO DROP THE DIME

Beyond the heavy crash of waves
assume only the possibility

      brilliant blue gray silver fog

            pages turning

                    Mexican rock & roll

Memory of waking up beneath the Venice pier
it is as it was
      by reason, shame & reverence
                    A Test of Poetry

FAKE BLONDE IN RED

A wind opens the door
the shattered sun
Mount Tamalpais drifting in the fog
the road to Dakar

It's the cool wind
coming in off the ocean
at dusk
the hills are on fire
I'm thirsty
this is an interpretive dance

By the silvery light of tidepools
I often think of the
tear-stained pavement
of Todos Santos
        Hawaiian mythology
              & all the names that are
                      crossed out in your address book

                        whoever you are this time

yr pearls, yr Mexican silver, yr troubled past
assuming a pale shade of
                variegated turquoise

but like alleyways
                near the beach
       held in the grip of
                a sunset aura
the burgundy nail polish
           was a dead giveaway

THEY CALL ME PAGLIACCI BUT MY REAL NAME IS MR. EARLE

All that I no longer am
yet carry w/me
an inheritance left unclaimed

        half buried in the sand
                half washed away in the tide

w/I suppose Oceanities of misappropriated
        albatross-befeathered
                shadow wings on the waves?

        Only the tender caress of oblivion
                can take the guesswork out of mercy
                        is another way I could have said it

but if I was talking to you I
wouldn't have to say a thing

THE PHONE IS RINGING
for Joanne Kyger

She said "Everyone deserves to be a bodhisattva
if only for one day"

But missing the evening of slack-key guitar at Pt. Reyes
due to television or immigrant authority or
elbows at the Food Bank
I suppose we should opt for a bag of rice
& some seaweed

"You might feel bad but you won't starve"

The "burden of opportunity" has a certain charm but
I'm not sure that it's the truth

These things must be sorted out

So many sand pebbles to choose from
agate, quartz, jade, glass, wood, iron, bone,
styrofoam—

I'll take the one that's shaped like my heart

Let me know when you've found it

CASUAL MYTHOLOGY

The Set-Up
Alchemical formulas
memorized from a lifetime of
Chinese take-out menus

one from column A, two from column B

        falling somewhere between
        "know thyself" & "roll your own"

Palm trees laying down a little shuffle-music

plus several tons of damp
not to mention suntan lotion

      rocked by waves of nightshade turquoise
      flickering like my heart

        all candle-lit & guided by voices

A Shade Past Turquoise
Ceremonies of sunset
& all the tarantellas of the coast

    more restrained, less
        dithyrambic than a Dirge

      The path down to the beach
      winding thru torch aloe & thistle
      being the lyric equivalent

& the light
as reflected off a warped mirror
    Etruscan or carnival-style
        spilling tidepools along the way

thus did I occasion the proverb
w/the usual consequence & valerian scripture

      if only to be the one who looks into yr eyes
      & lies to you

but beneath the wheels of Blakean rooftops
    & not far from a secret break I call Tombstones
a cool breeze ripples thru the eucalyptus
      - *wave crash, engines racing, hula music* -
if you listen real close I mean

99 Degrees
Not the way I would have played it
Sir Gawain & the Green Knight as much as
that other guy

a Minnie the Mermaid meets Marlon Brando kind of deal
w/Stagger Lee, The Golden Bough, & yr Magic Eight Ball
(just in case)
              parked out back of
                      Laocoön & Sons Surf Shop

canned laughter & larceny in the streets
unlikely to give the slightest hint of repurposed karma

but running the gamut from some
obscure theory of harmony
      to first-class accommodations & cocktails
          on the rainy balcony above
                the River of Forgetfulness

CONSPIRING TO HIJACK MY OTHERWISE DELICATE SENSIBILITIES

Wet streets
    glossy eyes
        lonely footsteps
lead or follow
        E-changing the paraphernalia of
any evidence to the contrary
    crossing the bridge between
            summer rain & revelation

as noted in the standard text

Light   & shadow   distributed among
            undersea flowers

compressed air   a ripple of regret

& then what?
        washed in seafoam

but begging indulgence
        without vows or refuge
    gazing out
        thru the windshield
into a kind of
        melted plastic Buddha-land
    where pickup trucks, motorcycles,
            & spaceships converge
gunning their engines beneath a
        sunset sky riding high above
like a slice of forever
        w/a limited shelf life

LIFTED FROM THE PROVEBS

The seabreeze
stepping it up in the
ancestral cypress
        stained-glass
            catching fire at sunset
    shark-tooth earrings & power tools
            shipped by seagull to Sumatra
      as in a biblical remix
        transmitted via a telepathic
            call & response system

The future of one moment
        vs the future of the next
    already packed into the
        big Cadillac of the past that
            never stopped to pick me up
    that summer afternoon
            hitch-hiking on the PCH

It was a *20,000 Leagues Under the Sea*
        meets *Sailing to Byzantium* situation
    w/seductive surf tattoo forensics
      adagio dancers
        & a squad of pelicans flying
            higher than love at first sight

no question about it

Yr heart is a framed portrait of the
wind riding in on a
            southwest swell, I said,
    & yr eyes are windows
        left open in the rain

REVEALING A FORMAL EXISTENCE INDEPENDENT OF THE RUSSET SKY

A long walk on a short pier

    a wetsuit allegedly blessed by the Pope

        a bent piece of lord have mercy

looming above

    yr heart   my heart   & the blank part

playing both ends
    against the middle
                just a half-
        breath away
                from the vacant
      lot behind the
           taco stand

& you can pretend you
          see yr reflection
  in the polished
      blue mirror of
            a summer's day
but it isn't yrs
      until you give it away

LONG PAST GONE

Ceremony
Bended knees & cracked radiator hoses
on the rusty side of the cypress grove

Lost in Translation
She sent me out for wine & roadmaps
& I returned w/workgloves & Mexican beer

Left Coast Bingo w/Top Spin
1. Falling down stairs
2. Never spilled a drop

LOADING HISTORY

You have to admire the
scope & scatter of it all
no matter which
side of the reflection you
find yrself on

the specific gravity of a rainy day
hanging in the balance

on the wing
                      winging it

w/rude awakenings
(late, lamented & conniving)
groaning across the two-lane blacktop
trucks of hassle & barrel
rolling transport

& the way it's all been pasted to
a page torn from the
dark gray sky
                    w/silver mists retrieved

building propensities

           circled by fate & the dotted line that
                yearns for yr signature

ACE OF TENTACLES
for Micah Ballard

I prefer the laughter of strangers
to the photo op I missed on purpose

as it may be the only remaining evidence
of an inner war of attrition

& livid w/ritual anomalies I could fake but
couldn't explain even if I wanted to

Ceremonies of crushed glass might ignite the
sea mist in somebody's dream

where I'm feeling conspicuously invisible
as always when I'm holding

THE NAME OF THE ROSE

The wind backs down the tide
picks up & we're no different

Time spins to the ground
& yr eyes are sand formations
constantly shifting   changing color
suffused in restless ocean gray shadows rippling
in pale sunlight

The mockingbird sings the same song but
in a higher register

& yr soul if it even exists
I couldn't say if any of us for certain but
something in the air anyway
besides this damp compression of tinsel mist
reaching down to rap its knuckles against the waves

or remember how someone else may have said it
& how easy it was to forget

THE THOMAS DE QUINCEY SHUFFLE

Painting myself into a corner
                         drenched in powder-blue light
                 w/a wisp of silver nitrate
like dengue fever
        shutting down a
                grounding session
                       on the open water it
pretends a finely manicured trigger finger
on its way to the local Earl Scheib's to get an
early Renaissance paint job
                 an accessory after the fact
coruscating in the late tide
Proteus to Kanaloa
          blue sparkle w/chrome inlay & the flatted fifth
                  pretending one was another
& when the light slices in the
                       shadows stretch out
             along the jangling
                 nerves & visionary swoons
of motorcycle cowboys
        across the rippling consciousness of a
                       syncopated bass line
dying in the feedback of
a distant riff

DEVOTIONS (AFTER RIMBAUD)

To Our Lady of Wet Sand
                resolute, inviolate
a garland of seaweed in her hair
—For the damp souls of the drowned

To Sister Yolanda Pipeline
           lighting matches
                  in the dark
—For children consumed by fever

To Long Tall Sally
           her bikini of corrugated steel
                  & the awkward flutter of her eyelashes
—For the unforgiven

To the revolutionary cadres of
                      Topanga, Malibu & Rincon

To the benediction of the tides
            anointed by salt spray & foam
ceremonies of beach concrete
                  w/the chrome-plated sun tilting down into
                              a tangle of shadows
—For those who have yet to lose their way

AT BOLINAS

Beach eucalyptus rattling its silver blades
understood by the bending mirrors of the tide
in a dyslexic translation from Latin
to neon
Kalifornia spelled with a "k" as in katatonic
& I'm rolling downhill backwards
reciting the 23rd Psalm (the
cantilever section)
but in the grip of madrigals & torch ballads
if only to say
"Shake the hand that shook the hand
of Charlie Manson & the Wu-Tang Clan"
expecting waves to descend from the sky
not to abbreviate surfboards but
the float switch approaching zero hour
when no one's looking
& having mastered the art of walking Spanish
I was uniquely qualified to spill a Bloody Mary
on your itsy bitsy teenie weenie
yellow polka dot kimono
leaving a stain shaped exactly like my life

SUZIE Q DOES THE ZOMBIE TWIST

Behind every dark night of the soul there's
a victimless crime w/yr name on it
& babies get tossed like kitchen
sinks from 8-story windows
only to land w/a thud in the middle of
yr violin solo

Expecting it all to rattle down into the sand
is one way to say it

clang. wiggle. crash. blink.
The Art of the Fugue

& the band plays & the road hums
inside a cloak of sea mist that
thins out as the sun climbs into a flat blue sky
as though it was a litmus test gone terribly wrong

You could always just chugalug a quart of Pennzoil
& go splashing thru puddles on the ocean floor
      listening to seagulls riffing on something
            Fats Navarro played in 1950
                  recorded a week before he died

& the wind shifts offshore to hollow out the waves
that Spring morning at Playa San Pedrito
as I drained the last of the tequila & w/numb fingers
unlaced my sneakers

Some things are given to you
while other things are taken away

IF I WROTE THIS IN TIJUANA 40 YEARS AGO WOULD I REMEMBER?

I'm wandering thru the long dark hallways of a
monastic 15th century labyrinth
looking for the alcove where they
keep the vending machines

& sifting thru reflections in a broken mirror
I lean out over the stone window ledge to gaze down upon
the ocean
          all tangled in conflicting tides all wrong
the waves all shattered
                w/milk-white foam folded into every corner

    (but then I may have been looking at the sky)

The wind kicks up it's cold this is the day I died

        I never but momentarily retain
            a pretense of having walked this far
                resisting like orchids in the rain
                    these defining moments

& don't peek but picture them where they drizzle
eternalized & extrapolated
as a heavy dose of early morning fog
wraps the coast in several shades of gray
not the least of which is green

MR. ZOG'S 3-DAY NOCTURNE

A dented fender of surf
a whiff of cheap perfume

    & maybe the heart is like a bus wreck
just outside Truth or Consequences, New Mexico
        where I could be carrying a specimen jar
containing a butterfly, some seashells,
& 6 bottlecaps

mementos of X-ville Beach

It was never a question of where I was going
but how I would get there

    rolling past palisades of howling palm trees
       & swamp-water lagoons of puddles that
stretch from once upon a time
       to the long goodbye

It goes without saying & then some
if one hopes to get any kind of traction
i.e., credit for time served

    & without the charm of a doubt
the risk inherent
       in the glittery parts

as fog drops the shade on a
flawless wave
that traveled all the way from Hong Kong
in the back seat of a gleaming turquoise
Cadillac convertible

BLACK OPS
for Jimmy Dunagan

The countdown (backwards):
The Jewel of Denial
The Breeze & I
The Man at the Table
    (didn't necessarily look like Joan Crawford with a beard)
Francois Villon

      A story told in 300 Hawaiian shirts

           Different names for inconvenient body parts

There you are
& there you go

"thine true heritage"

beneath the big California sky which I know you
depend upon as much as I & gaze up into it when nothing else
makes sense
        as thankfully so little does
    cloudy or clear

BACH'S *TOCCATA & FUGUE IN D MINOR* VS THE BELAIRS *MR. MOTO* (NOT IN COMPARISON BUT UNDER PERFECT CONDITIONS)

Palace
Pantages
Palladium

Bali Ha'i

A bird, a fish, a pope
on horseback

                Dragonfly visiting the
                torch aloe prickly pear cactus
                blue agave corner of the beach

or the Garden of Epicurus
is my seashell

THE SCENE OF THE CRIME

It wasn't easy balancing on one foot
in front of the firing squad but
it all came together at the right time

like drifting thru fog on the moon

or learning how to duck dive

Back then I drove an El Camino
that looked like a pterodactyl
& when you slid in beside me
the sky caved in

300 miles later we bought some tacos
it was Thursday or something
& I hadn't eaten in a year

LET THERE BE LITHIUM

The moist, dislocated air
all parlance & midnight
bought & paid for w/an ounce of
ocean haze
              plus or minus the
sharkskin wetsuit
        w/room for paranoia & glorification

but tenderly & w/total disregard & leaky pipes
to interrogate the looming amoeba w/trick questions
in pantomime

Break me off a piece of a day drenched in the
golden light of Autumn, *por favor*
where slick waves crash & the sun drags a string of
rusty cans over a horizon that
went out of business sometime during the Bronze Age

I've been here before but not like this
expecting wisdom to replace the white powder in my blood
any minute now

the twisted silverware harkening back to that
heaven of the Jews
obscured by the fog that pulls Santa Cruz out to sea

the wind sweeping in off the water whispering
"Let us pray. . ."

but it was always locals only
which meant God wasn't invited

THE LAST CAR THAT PARKED HERE IS STILL MISSING

Everything is tumbling past
a steel guitar I had at first thought
looked like rain

The trial of true redemption slips a little
in the Chinese transliteration
                skimming the silver
                      torched by blossoms

      a way to compensate for those
            rogue mermaids on horseback

not to mention Thor Heyerdahl, Sister Aimee Semple,
& Miki's lush beehive?

Your brain seems to be on an extended vacation, a sea cruise,
maybe a world tour, including every empty parking lot from the
Forbidden City to Tierra del Fuego. Factor in the long way around
& you just might make it back by suppertime.

NEXT TIME I'LL BUILD YOU A MAI TAI

The lordly & isolate satyrs
shop at discount stores
& go to ball games
I may have passed them
on the road
I was probably riding the clutch
while running the raw footage
beneath a pinwheel sun
the radio tuned to static
a kind of white noise for a blue day
drenched in radiance & apprehension
testing the pulse of
Spanish guitars strumming the
latitude & longitude of a crooked smile
waiting for you to
hurry the plot to the inevitable
exit thru the gift shop
& you might find me in the parking lot
observing a psychosomatic
minute of silence
one diligent eyelash away from
donating my sunglasses to science

MANCHURIAN SPACE REGGAE

The gas heater performs a little
Erik Satie
at 3 in the morning

parsed in sonic platitudes
real life isn't all that different

A soft summer breeze whistles
doom & entanglements

& you recognize too late
you're on the verge of becoming the
perfect stranger

CONFLICT RESOLUTION AMONG THE MOUTH BREATHERS

She wanted to know the preliminary
parts of whatever
empty rules of heaven
& though I was convinced it had
more to do w/coconut milk & tequila than
the gnostic scriptures
I just couldn't see how she could
drive that truck all the way there & back
w/a leaky head gasket & no muffler
but like cutting forever in half
w/the sky behind smoked glass
& bongo windchimes knocking in the
late afternoon seabreeze
further is just about as far as you can go

DANCING TO ELEVATOR MUSIC IN THE STAIRWELL

Zooming in on those
dollface coordinates (lipstick
on the fender)

It was a case of
         what you believe versus
     what you set fire to
             in the backyard

She begs to differ the
         clip-on sunset fading like a
     last kiss & the bounce
            a bump that coaxes madrigals
from the shake & bake sky

        No comfort to take & none given

what we know
put to better use
w/a casual glance of downward
     I want to say disdain
         or is it compassion for the dead
the homage of incessant obligation
     & all the immaculate alibis
         cut from the same damp cloth

You can always pry the label off
& start over
         while Heartfelt Achilles
     & the Jukebox Transfusion hold sway

& I could see it in yr eyes
dividing three octaves four ways

FINDING THE LOST CHORD ON A PLASTIC SOUVENIR UKULELE

I Think I Woke Up in Laguna Niguel
Delusions of grammar
vs the exact square footage of
The Cantos

Listing to Starboard
Lewis MacAdams said that the
hardest part about being a poet
is being a poet

So Noted
A mourning dove in the yard
3:35 pm   *la paloma*

A GUIDE TO SELF-MEDICATION

I've heard that the giant squid is a notorious amnesiac, swimming aimlessly out into the remote reaches of the Pacific, never remembering where it came from or why, transported into Asiatic scenes, affected by ancient, monumental, cruel & elaborate religions, the vast empires also in which parakeets, beluga whales & eternal pyramids drift among reeds & antediluvian mud w/bells & positraction, & all of it less than a shadow's depth on wet pavement

YOU'D BETTER HAVE A PLAN B
for Edward Dorn

The onshore breeze as articulated by
Big Sur windchimes
    at 4:19 in the after
    noon the
        sunlight coming in at an
            autumnal slant

    Did you notice? I didn't until just now
        the surging ocean waves paved for sunset

My troika was pursued by wolves
but I do have an assortment of acrylic paints
& the gravitas of an Obi Wan Kowalski or
Baba O'Riley

    Tripping the light fantastic they used to say

        playing against type

It will either inspire
    prophetic dreams
    or leave you stranded in a
        dark corner of yr mind
begging for more
    like I said to my gal Sappho
        the first one's free but
            I'm seeing double

SECOND-HAND SMOKESCREEN

1
A light blue light
                        slides in off the sea
           the early morning mist
                               slowly lifts
        a duet for three voices
& by noon I'm lost in the chord changes
of another tune
                   tapping on the pavement
w/a spoon

2
           The wind lays it down
                     on a B bender
as the tide shifts   out where
   light blue light & dark conspire
6:32 am   in the year of our lord
        & it's too soon for love to
                         change its tune

3
The early morning mist is
      like a primer gray Chevy
              parked at the beach & I'm
pretending it's the wind
                   sliding in off the sea
that keeps me in love's
            light blue light
     which by noon is worth its weight in
silver spoons
          tapping on the lid of the tide

WHERE HAVE ALL THE PAYPHONES GONE

The Wizard of Oz wasn't a wizard at
all, but a little guy named Oscar who
had a glass eye & a knack for the short
con
        knocked around Venice Beach w/a hunch-
back named Vera
                operating in & around a phone
booth outside the Fox Theater on Lincoln
Blvd circa 1971 or so

A few years later . . . nowhere to be found

yr guess as good as mine

I moved north to Half Moon Bay in '76
the phone booth went away two decades after that

The Fox Theater was converted to an
indoor swap meet which
is pretty much what it was
any night when the lights went down
& the screen lit up
& a drowsy numbness was dealt out in dime bags

REVVING IT UP BETWEEN SU TUNG-P'O & THE NOTEBOOKS OF SHELLEY

Dancing with the Starfish
A coastal extravaganza starring
Odysseus, Ishmael, 27 seasick mermaids
& an octopus named Mustang Sally

1971
If I could remember that far back
I wouldn't admit it

Metaphysical Therapy
I'm down with the mysteries of the universe
"You walk in the front & walk out the back"
Just don't fuck with my car

SKIMMING THE SURFACE

Warm light leaking in thru
Venetian blinds
                    warmer if I step out into it
flickering light & shadow in the leaves
                        patterns I'd like to remember

Japanese maple   shades of green   deep blue sky

along w/several popular bird songs
                - warble, chirp, trill, squawk -

relayed by Aristophanes, Alfred Hitchcock, or

2
If I were ever to write an autobiography
it would have to be about someone else

        Where are we November
                    El Día de los Muertos
            furiously hitting the vape pipe
                        fast & loose

the early morning fog mist
the gut-wrenching zeal
the revolving door of the confessional

            St. Augustine or Thomas de Quincey

puttering around various conflicts of interest
on the way to the Tropicana Motel

3
That was me then
            a punchline ending in patchouli
        lead-weights in my sneakers

                        Where was I Topanga
or Chichén Itzá

                knee deep in the parking lot

watching wet footprints evaporate
on the sun-bleached pavement

DROP C TUNING FOR STEAM-DRIVEN GUITAR

Built to Specifications w/Lyric Torque
& Dual Exhaust
That cloud skating across the sky
      seems to have been
           thrown into reverse
     like a little pink tractor
              hauling in another
                    postcard sunset

orange, blue, & a different sort of
green
      filtering down thru every
           worn out welcome
                riding in on the ocean breeze

A Hazard to Navigation
Any moment I could be there listening
or right here not listening but
hearing it all tumble
in one ear & out the other

                - an unobstructed view -

     hither & tither
     to & fro   pretty much
     hither & yon   in other words
                       like they say

       "The weather will change"

How can it not be now?

Wired for Sound
      Bridging the gap between
          what you want & what you need

                        I would if I could

Staggering among shadows & words I can't pronounce
            words I can't quite reach although
                        I know what they look like
& where they might fit in a poem
                                    setting the hook

        just saying so is a kind of singing

Tone Deaf
The wind kicks up late
            stirring the
                        eucalyptus kool-aid
                                    is one way to say it
though my head is bent on the
rhyme implied
                        which could be enough to
                        change someone's tune

& not necessarily set to music because
what is music?
                        Other than
                                    vibrating
                                                molecules of air

            & at what frequency in the mind
                        when words are not read out loud
still renders a
                        tone & rhythm & shape
                                    as much in image as sound

you listen to it w/a flashlight

Another Damp Interlude Tapping Out
Morse Code Jazz
            These are the High Holy Days

68

Feast of St. Tarzan
       & Duke Kahanamoku

Perimedes & Eurylochus

      the Warne Marsh Trio
            the Thelonious Monk Quartet
        Art Tatum working thru *Stompin' at the Savoy*

Mexico City Blues

      The books are within easy reach
      as is the grain

Shimmying Down the Stations of the Breath
An electric 12-string seabreeze
         strumming the drumroll sand

     zoom bop rock & rail

or whatever else claims that resonance
      so that yr little heart flips
          maybe spins off a pirouette

A Pantomime in Church Latin
w/Doc Holliday & Arthur Rimbaud
Leading to some
     heavy lifting
         in the echo chamber

Love is Not a Dream Returning
Allegory as Evidence
     Metaphor - not a brick wall but
         as a transparency like
window glass & can you
          sometimes see a reflection?
R E C O G N I T I O N

"The Poems"
    a preference for vowel sounds
           vs lead-based grammar
but the music intrinsic
    valves, gears, & hinges
           as rhyme could be Memory
of phrase or Image & where/how it turns
is that
    but say it like you mean it
a spillover from the Higher Mysteries
      Her eyes are the color of bourbon
   in a glass
       w/the light streaming thru it

PIER PRESSURE

Everything is as easy as it sounds
although it may result in liver disease

        If I could remember the combination to
        the tidepools at Agate Beach would it
        even the score?

Always the minute
detail as perhaps these palm
        trees instinctively predict the apocalypse
        (do you think?)

              & though my gods are crooked & maimed
I'm certain they must hold the clue
                deep red, black, silver & blue

I THOUGHT TO ROLL UP MY SLEEVES BUT THE LIGHT HAD BEEN ENCRYPTED & MY TATTOO DIDN'T TRANSLATE

The sky above us is
            whispering (blue)
      softly dusted w/silver haze
sworn to green scenes
                      right out of the tide book
          w/bubbles & like glistening
              catalogs of subtropical flowers
                  printed on
                          silk sleeves of fog

If I wasn't there you'd have to
dream up someone else to talk to someone
else who wouldn't listen because the song the
wind sings in the eucalyptus is cranked up to
10 on the voodoo dial & if you had wings
you'd probably make a similar sound

            shadows spilling
                onto the sidewalk

                You can read yr future there

                      & I had to ask but
                          you didn't
                              have to answer . . .

For every door that opens another closes

        & now the sky is melting
                      like a box of crayons
in the Painted Desert
              riding in on the
         shattered chrome drainage
                  at the drop edge of yonder

ROLL BOUNCE

Launch Angle
Walking in on flames
like Mayakovsky
w/a dog named Snake Eyes

Moving Pictures
Hawaiian music w/rack & pinion steering
crisscrossing the gray whale migration route
on Samurai Sunday
                                The variorum edition
revving its engine in the
                alley behind Tattoo Tacos
    in deference to anyone who can
                    pick up a frying pan
& you're tapping at the glass
          asking if they can turn up the volume

Miles Runs the Voodoo Down
A delicately threaded
                          ripple of smoke
            bends to reach & exit
                 thru the open window

flesh
snags
consciousness

                Money from home

40 OUNCE BLUES

The sky bends into flickering neon
& the tuning fork lays down a
weary doo-wop
reminding me of how warm the pavement could be
at night in Ocean Park
          the summer of 1975
                released on yr own recognizance

In dreams I return to those places
        that are still haunted by the shadow of
            who I was & I double-down

There are bigger mistakes to be made
along w/more interesting
consequences

      if one means to be the least bit accurate

as it would be conjecture
                creating the illusion

finding love in the parking lot
              the radio tuned to static
      dry leaves blown skittering
                across the blacktop

      The supplication & the statistical anomalies
          dissolving in the mist of former expectations

I wasn't listening but I heard every word

like bingo night
at the Time Warp Motel
      where the sign reads "VACANCY"
& blinks

                    off & on
to remind you
                          tiny bubble notes
                          from a long way off

                                            each bubble contains a word

TORCH BALLAD W/A MENTHOL FILTER

You were wearing yr getaway pearls
& I was charting alternate routes to bliss
singing "Baby let me follow you down"
like Orpheus
                         undone by those wet kisses
as though it was the full tide
                reading from The Book of Mumbles
or a 30-page haiku
      w/chrome hubcaps
                putting a dent in my bloodshot RayBans
as I step across yr four-lane balcony
                  w/a six-pack of adrenaline
                            & a one-track mind
& when you lip-synch the Minuet in G
      I nod out like a 14th century pope
            ordering the taco plate at Las Palmas
w/the beach tilted in the fog
    like a bikini in the refrigerator
sweating out the last
                day of summer

I HEAR A SYMPHONY

The music of her eyes

an underwater saxophone
diminished in the tide

"What's yr music like?"

A disco ball eaten by a chainsaw

Do you really want to know?

SHINE A LIGHT

Somewhere in the wind where
a sigh could be mistaken for a
ripple thread of prophecy

(fake right, go left)

A Social & Economic History of Poetry
sifting down thru the grillwork of heaven
tossing an anchor out the passenger window

I've heard that song too

        The homage paid w/interest compounded

A thermal inversion or some other
        atmospheric eccentricity
                strumming every heart-shaped molecule

        Drifting sand & low-end torque
            snare drums & Ave Marias
                (except she meant every word of it)

I wouldn't know from
where I part the drizzle
but if you run the numbers you
could probably make it work

        The waves all blown out late in the
        afternoon w/the wind & that
                precious blue reflecting
        back off the dark
                sheet-metal sky

PAINTING SHADOWS

One born of sea foam
may just as well have been born on a bus
careening thru the dark at midnight
in the rain. Her lips were
pale at dawn. I made a distinction
when I should have
shut the fuck up. The sky mixing
shades of gray as yet
undefined. The color of pearls I think
was her answer thus born of sea
foam & darkness beneath the waves.
The moon a coin in her hand she
flips it to predict the tides.
Once the hours hollowed out it was
carried on the wind to
carve its trace as a lustrous
sphere. I swallowed two & held my breath.
The bus was pulling into the stop.
It was noon.

FROM A MOTEL ROOM IN VENICE
for Pamela

A hit man w/a habit
Gerard de Nerval
sheets of sunlight

I was thinking about Malibu I guess

Cerveza San Lucas

negotiating the skateboard traffic
& the hysterical adobe
Travels in Abyssinia & the Harar

We are Beyond Broke
the check's in the mail
minus any photographic evidence, alas

Blue nada & the midnight echo

after so many miles how can you be sure

Duncan breaks the filter off
"The only way you can taste the tobacco"
I had forgotten

You wouldn't have recognized me
nor I you in the glare of that Pacific blade
loyal to the ocean & "The Poems" as ever

recalibrating the *Bright Star* sonnet as Leweye said
& the beauty of that moment among the voices, Pamela

"We think there is a soul but
we don't know"

DROPPING IN ON A FLOATER

Invoking the pink & green
gods responsible for this pale
sunlight
I could envision a future where
a drizzle of misdirection
would be my ticket to the
wisdom, detachment & compassion that
would come to define my later years

I used to think so

& remember the way the late
afternoon light fell thru the eucalyptus
trees on the bluff above the beach
& those pragmatic butterflies

There was a time I'd have known
exactly when to
vault the fence & hit the water
before anyone knew or cared
& I struggled with that burden

even so tempting fate I had to
settle for a percentage of the take

footprints in wet sand
trembling velvet tides bagged & tagged
& those cold blue flames under the sea
like a crash course in Taoist alchemy

BENDING LIKE A SPOON TO THE FLAME

Her Favorite Color is Sunset
She was splashing thru the shallows
at the deep end
       & I was hydroplaning past the odd
                Latin phrase that
can't be translated

The light was endless
but it didn't have anything to do w/us
holding up our end of eternity

       Catch it later
           on the playback loop
    beneath a pale green sky
             tilted in such a way the
rust-bucket haze slides off into
         episodes of stained glass

High & Low
The song seeps in
    blue-eyed green-eyed turquoise black
and (and) (and)
         dripping mist on the beach
at Pleasure Point

Custom shapes & guitar solos
     taking us out past the breakwater
        past the reef & into the
           Echo Chamber

I'm guessing the door is always open
bajo las olas

& that silver shuffle
        leaning into the skid
                wouldn't surprise me if it did

To the Gods of Medicine & Ding Repair
A flicker of light maybe
        far out at sea
               to float the memory

        She used to say it that way
                on the embarcadero
beneath a tropic sky
        the same color as 40 links of chain
w/mudslide tremors & gaited horses
                out where the coast road veers off into
                        Bohemian rhapsodies

& that wingless per diem where
        sea meets sky in the
                pretense & the vapor
doesn't necessarily ring a bell
anywhere but here

EXILE ON BEACH STREET

You thought you could
                leave the dead behind but
    they follow you
                        as voices
                   in the choir of memory
belting out a few
            golden oldies

        although the needle
                   keeps skipping

& the fogmist tastes like
tequila
shipped in from Japan

HONG KONG BLUES

A combination of small south & northwest groundswells delivers waves of up to five feet at north-facing beaches where palomino seahorses gallop in the foam the thunder of their hooves no more than a whisper now as I gather a bouquet of broken glass & rusty windchimes for the French girl with leukemia who at this very moment is gently knocking at my door.

WALKING TIPTOE THRU THE RUINS OF WESTERN CIVILIZATION (W/HEADPHONES ON)

The rolling dark rocking
deep green turquoise steel
& corrugated foam

which from here resembles the warped
pages of a water-damaged book
the inscription illegible
a map of veins that have burst within
a bouquet of suicide morning glories

pale shades of azure & rust
left standing in the sun too long got bleached out

apothecary jars full of tepid
sunset & homegrown paleontology
eventually get profound

but it wasn't supposed to go down that way

How long before yr chosen
mirror reflects that tender urgency
& reluctance

raining down power chords
like a black pajama death wish
on the slow train to the Hollywood Laundromat

TIJUANA GIFT SHOP

Klo-rene
If you listen close to those
windy palm trees
you can hear the soft
        whisper of what could be
                a rockslide out at the
                        edge of yr neural system
but is more likely just a
        clever born-again hula doll
                tenderly scooping out yr brains
                w/a backhoe

The same amped eyeshadow & disregard applies
as love at first sight gets
bumped from the menu
leaving you to calculate the
rate of descent

        silk sunlight a go-go
        capsized in a sea of shadows

                the late afternoon sky vs "The Poems"
                in a brown paper bag

Running Up the Score
I could never see the percentage in
dealing in the sacraments
but then I'm always cutting corners
                ready to pop the clutch
        & fishtail up the coast highway
            behind the wheel of a
                      working hypothesis

True redemption may be
                only a step away but

    it's the step after that
                          could get you DQ'd

both do whispers w/considerable
                           je ne sais quoi
baptized into one body

        but there's a place we can go
                        bypassing the relays
a place just outside yr comfort zone
where the last black lagoon under the sea turns blue
& the fog echoes in silver

I Left My Feet in My Other Shoes
(for Bill Berkson)
Those shades of blue in the ocean haze
only exaggerate the emptiness of the
washed-out sky

                a hybrid Day of the Dead tattoo
                      fading into a sunburnt shoulder

Bumpy weather minus the disconnect of
rambling bird notes
rising above the shifting tides

        diesel sand driven beneath the foam
                measured in intervals like beach tar

I could still feel the
                kelp-bed tremors & cold knuckles
the deep blue nomenclature & ringtone
                      resurrecting a phantom pain
& then I remembered that I always wanted to
end a poem with the word
"polyurethane"

ALIEN VS PREDATOR, OR THE LAST DAYS OF DISCO

I knew I must have been blessed because I managed to step in every puddle between here & Front Street. She was there when I got back & it was easy to see why she stood sideways with her sisters in every snapshot pasted into her family's photo album. The engines in her eyes were designed for another purpose, one that had yet to be exploited. Her neon lip gloss gave every word she said a luminous presence that made me think of the lights along the pier on a foggy night.

A TWOFER AT THE FIVE & DIME

Transparent reflections on the window glass
are reminders of the illusory nature of existence

A dusting of clouds in the beach sky

No one notices how the color changes but it does

Green, pink, orange, & blue
which is strange for this time of year
when pearls & moths should be the prevailing hue

Other colors are playing mahjong & smoking Pall Malls

going to El Segundo, metaphorically

RIDING A PIANO INTO THE UNKNOWN

The sun skids along the
edge of the ocean haze
recalling the specific gravity
of a rainy day
& the five-finger discount

Street scenes out of Ovid
& I don't know but drifting
like a shipwreck in a bottle

& I must enter again the
cathedral of vaulted Pacific steel
buttressed w/seaweed & foam

prayer wheels spinning
like flying saucers getting dizzy
the invasion postponed

RIFFLE SHUFFLE

Reverse Meditation
I was languishing between the
bubble of her apprehension
& *A Long Hard Look at Psycho*

The 3-Second Rule
She said I was transparent but
it didn't mean that she could
see right thru me

Dividing Now from Forever
1. That's her speed-shifting on Mulholland Drive
2. That's me in the headlights

SLIDING DOWN THE LADDER OF A
TRUE BELIEVER BEFORE THE LIGHT CHANGES

Being now at an age in
which the
tattered coat fits
                loosely rather
                          Byzantine
the numbered days
        even those w/out numbers
                stagger on
somehow
        soon to be forgotten

      The least silken but
               reed-brown greens of
        kelp-lit eyes & secret
                    watery extensions
thereby assembled like an
ancient alphabet
      whistling past the
               singing school

Who needs poetry

        It's a statement
               not a question

One song or
        another to
    sing along with
                    the voice (yr
own) is familiar
        though out of reach a
moment within
        some fine isolated verisimilitude
      as if to memoir-map the psalms & sutras that

never made it onto my bingo card

           a lateral presence
                   to be present
              in as much as
                          held in the mind
  however
                one could phrase it so

It's heartening to know that
any word can become meaningless
if used correctly

            You look for the "tell"
                   in the poet's eyes
              having flunked the personality test

A quick glance back
over yr shoulder

            Scylla on the jagged rocks
                Charybdis the whirlpool

Odysseus had ignored the signs

            I would never assume to
                     connect the dots

& even if I didn't say what I mean
the words mean what they say

words
        like windows you can
     see thru
            climb thru
                    leap or fall from

& so across the wet
        hollow stone steps that
                lead to fog plumes
          & forgetfulness

murky & indistinct
streaming neural movies that were a hit
back in the Pleistocene

the sun racing across the
shallow sky
        like a '69 Chevy Malibu
      encased in amber

spinning the wheels is customary

      but whistling it backwards
            standing outside the
                bait shop in the rain
     w/a surfboard & a flashlight
   susceptible to the incidental
            revery not to mention arias
& freight train blues
        spot welded to a fender of
    midwinter beach logistics

& the light
like a borrowed kimono falling onto the sand
bending the way the sky does
      above the cypress & eucalyptus that
            rake the concrete w/shadows
       articulated by the seabreeze

MIXING UP THE MEDICINE

Some of us walk away,
skip, leap, or fall

skidding around corners that
just aren't there

force of habit no doubt
laying down impossible odds
but I just don't know . . .

put a dollar sign on something when I die

Paradise goes thud
topped with garnished wages
& bowling trophies

Meanwhile he set aside his
labor-intensive epiphanies
& attended to the dumpster fire that
was left holding the bag

soft exit spun 180 degrees Hello?
beyond high or hope

all the price tags end in 99 cents

SUBLIMINAL CUTBACK

One False Move Deserves Another
I don't think I'll ever write a decent sonnet
until I learn how to stutter

Tunneling Thru the Dreaded "Maybe"
on a Blank Tuesday
Take yr time
whatever time it takes
try to sing along

Readymade Dreams & the Voluptuous
The rarefied air
Rare   Fried   Air
Heat Wave
Fond memories of delirium
teetering on the edge of my lo & behold

THE ZEN OF WEARING SUNGLASSES AT THE MOVIES

If you can remember it, then
it probably didn't happen

a careful nod to the best laid plans

        as it could be a footnote to the
Parable of the Gringo
                (had too much to drink
                        or maybe not enough)

A tropical aura
in a long black kimono
                vs a diminished chord
          in B-flat minor

but lifting the cellophane
                        off the tide
        beneath the wheels of El Paradiso
a haze of smog lingers
in yr eyes
                heavily redacted
      by dawn's early light

A DIFFERENT DYNAMIC

11 heads
2 arms
1 head
1000 arms   *& a mustache*
1 head
8 arms
        – Philip Whalen

BENEATH THE FORTUNE PALMS by Kevin Oxydol
    "We need something to replace the old gods"
        she said & I suggested a package of *Gauloises*

CLASSICAL RHETORIC FOR THE MODERN STUDENT by
Kevin Obstacle
    Her faraway eyes haunt my tidewater reckoning

LOW-TIDE LOW-LIFE by Kevin Oxidados
    I'm burying sunlight in wet sand
        as she dances across the beach towards me
            in the here-to-forever
                leadpipe coastal haze

PLAYING THE PERCENTAGES

The day a dusty

                                              gray w/a

                  hint of

                          rose

                                                  & those

                    nameless shades

insurgent

                          swept in the slow

       tide

                                    approximating the

                  speed dreams

                                            of the tortoise

tending to collateral

                          What is known is

                              out to lunch

      blank echoing dark & empty

                                  it is what it is

flickering, light

                          except at night

                                        Let it ride

              (independent suspension)

                  "The heart has its reasons that
                  reason knows not of"

Honolulu Baby

                      where'd you get those eyes

(THEY CALL THE WIND) CHOLITA

Wet sand
diving beneath the waves
& what could be mistaken for a dark white piece of the sky

    Lots of air the ocean the
                      highway hugging the coast

Places along the way: line assumes a shape a memory
1. Moby Taco   panoramic & in technicolor
2. Desolation Surf Shop   (my dreams are seldom
3. Sunset Liquors   black & white) every
4. Brew, Chew & Spew   footstep, wing-flap, fin-splash
5. Medicine Man's Drive Thru
6. Tidewater Auto Body   kelp blossom
7. Tiki-Time Hawaiian Burgers
8. Snug Harbor Gas & Go   Beer can
9. Pacific Pipe & Forge

                      The Book of Revelations
                      in a grass skirt

THE SMOG'S VIBRANT GOWN

Beauty or not a recompense
my compass
                  "a paper moon above a cardboard sea"
& so forth
          in a homemade hazmat suit

odds & evens   (love assumes)   shadow games

as if to tip a hand
already played

              the same turning back the same
                      parting of the reeds

& the fog unfurls
inspiring dewy-eyed parking lot rhapsodies
held together w/duct tape & rhyme
lifted like a chalice rag
to be folded neatly & tucked away in a
dark green corner of the surf

somewhere in the region of Petey Wheatstraw
or Emily Dickinson

              but w/heavy waves rocking the pier the
swagger & stoke of it
                w/the passing of parochial time
& the countdown 10, 9, 8, 7-come-11 . . .

Ask for what you want
blink & it's gone
who knows where it comes from desire

LOWERING THE BOOM

Sedan Delivery
The sky flickering above the sea
or the memory of such
invites a casual witness

The decidedly distracted sunlight
wobbling like a Sumo wrestler
on stilts

The initial "thud" made possible if not
plausible
w/itemized deductions

I Saw the Movie & Read the Book
Escaping fate a lost cause
               tapping the pause button repeatedly
      The purest of smoke rings
                   measuring the wingspan

Hold Tight
A late winter afternoon
bending in the wind
             like a spring-loaded Shangri La
        in the cradle of Nowhere

GOING THE DISTANCE

The leaves all golden now
wasted

        lace-like skeletons of
            butterfly wings

"Why seek ye the living
among the dead?" they ask

                as well they should

      hovering between the
           bright cold flame of heaven
& the last recording of the
Memphis Jug Band

WHAT'S YOUR METAPHOR?

The fading mango sky
        is more than enough to
                burn out a few
                        neurotransmitters

though the small print contradicted
all claims thereby

                      five will get you ten

      straight up or out

             wouldn't necessarily
                change the tune

but working with & against the flow
hitting it sideways
        & cradled in that satin glow your
                eyes catch the light like
      a fistful of Andalusian needles
            smuggled in from
                    submarine realms of
                            rust & ruin
    scheming an elegant
    introspection
            adding by subtraction

a tiptoe samba
      across the wet sand
            vs a narcoleptic episode
                    for two

NICE CATCH

Her voice
approaching like
a high fly ball
hit to deep center field

I have to fade back
flip down the shades
reach back feel
for the fence

& leap—

Yes, I would
like another
cup of
coffee

thank you

3,000 CROOKED MILES TO HONOLULU

High Noon
The sun a soft
blossom the
color of hepatitis

Syllables of Passage
yet to be charted
whispered across the
ivory concordance of foam

Mood Indigo
Somewhere between
blue & violet
in the visible spectrum
as orchestrated by Duke Ellington

As Above, So Below
The sky was soaked in gasoline
& all I had to do was
strike a match

ROLL ME A PEARL

M'sieur Tarzan Buys a Record Player
The fog rolls in
right on time
& it's enough to make you
    kick up the high-beams
      on yr Manson lamps
   burning a hole thru all that
        damp nothing

"Why not" just hangs there
like a seagull
swimming unexpectedly
into this poem
      applying the weight of
   a single feather
       to the tone arm
as the Flying Burrito Brothers
    reinvent Dharma transmission
  as a 3-speed
    w/a Hurst shifter

Skip Trace
I said everything I know I
learned at the movies
but I didn't mean it that way

When the late show ends the
    detour takes us thru Pismo Beach
      by way of Kathmandu

Dense fog laden w/salt spray
& methylmercury

    voices in the eucalyptus—

                the slightest
                                breeze
                        starts a
                                new conversation

but words are only a
        part of what's being said

The Bitter Angels of Our Nature
The forest primeval
                The Florist of Evil
        (Baudelaire?)

Bela Lugosi in *Island of Lost Souls*
                        Morphine *Like Swimming*

Manzanita   Seaweed   Fuchsia

Nasturtiums clinging to beach pavement

not as it is
                but as it really was
                                back in reality
                susceptible to moods swings
                        & mile-long shadows

She said, "I'd hate to say I told you so"
& then she did

Roll Me a Pearl
I was paddling thru the shallows
waiting for the tide
        & you were cascading vertically on the beach
                as did St. John of the Cross
                        before he rusted out

the single-fin aesthetic notwithstanding

                  tilted mist   imaginary whispers

blue   green   & dark

          The rush of foam across the sand
                                    an immersive program

                tiny bubbles

I drew a blank shaped like the Great Coral Reef
              it didn't quite remind me of you
        or the money to be made
                       installing stained-glass windows
            in the shorebreak

Such passion is like a delicate flower w/bruised knuckles
        like an octopus tapdancing in a tidepool
            like a Spanglish translation of Catullus
                  parked outside the fantasy camp

something no one will ever remember
or forgive

THE OBLITERATION OF THE SELF
AS EVIDENCED IN WITTGENSTEIN'S SURF
ALMANAC

Whatever it was I saw dancing
in yr eyes
may have been left tied to a
kitchen chair in Tijuana

lost or defiant
but never both at the same time

You wore that halo like a crash helmet
& I drove w/one eye on the road
one eye on you
& the other eye on the
vows that failed us both

SURFING BY CANDLELIGHT

I tripped over my first bloody nose
& landed here
57 years later
beneath a dark sky getting darker
clabbering up to rain

& I played that clawhammer ukulele
like a champ
just so you'd know what it felt like

It was late summer on the coast
& you were like a brain surgeon
smuggling a pipe bomb
into my most cherished memories

AN OUNCE OF NIGHTINGALE
VS BANJOS IN THE EUCALYPTUS

The Wind Teasing a Song Out of the
Bent Cypress
        reaching for the pulse
                of rock & roll

Oddly Similar to What I Heard on Pier
Street in Hermosa Beach circa 1974
(odd only because I remembered it)

The Leaves are Full of Voices
& not unlike those in the
Greek Anthology
        but it wouldn't hurt to
                read the footnotes

RETRACING THE STEPS OF A LAST TANGO & MY HESITATION TO BAIL ON THE SCENE

Be assured there is a
ghostly presence
    whatever else is going on
  which is never enough it seems

     nothing ever really is

I don't know was it the guy who
wrote that book about Dionysus?

   Whoever it was they
    should have known better

Everything looks as though it's
  been parked in a tidepool aquarium for
several months
     & then hung out to dry
  in the remedial breeze

It's all within walking distance
    the hunchback palm trees,
      the rattling dead thistle, the
  yellow leaves that have their own light
as I'd like to think we all do but
      wait until after midnight

a roach of intrigue
  factoring in all the
    relentless details

   just a little something to
    set alongside the
      octopus in the bathysphere

as if you could pick & choose yr demons

The girl w/the Māori tattoo
for example
       replacing my heart
              w/a stolen hood ornament

Her hair was dark
& her eyes may have been the color of
Oaxacan jade
              forgotten now in the
                  neon repose of tides
because you can't
pay for the same crime twice

CARMEN & THE DEVIL RIDE A MULE THRU A FIELD OF POPPIES

Hearing Allen Ginsberg
yelling in my ear
like Ben Gazzara
in a John Cassavetes movie

& the hitchhiker Rio Bravo ghost leans in
looking more like Percy Bysshe Shelley
than John Wayne

It was time for time to run out
a clever plot device

        Mexican rooftops
            tilted in the rain

but the thing itself
      the sustain   (to be continued)
so as to leave an echo or to
        plant an echo in its place

      a rare occurrence in the currency
      & then some

Coral, sapphire, agate & jade
    are the prevailing
               colors of the day
fluttering in pale gray mist
        speed-shifting on the
PCH near Zuma
     where the tide plays "Topsy"
              on a drainpipe

WEARING YESTERDAY LIKE TOMORROW

We're still learning the
shape the sky takes
inside jagged cumulus
smoke-rings of haze
& broken shadow wings that
rake the sand

                    negative space
                            to the trained eye
part of the process
      (the one that got away)

Low-flying hosannas
w/unlimited mileage
tracing zig-zag tracks

more than enough (less than expected)

We call the row of empty bottles
dead soldiers
although the battle has yet to begin

TEA FOR TWO MINUS ONE & COUNTING

A 360 Off the Pipe
I was nodding out over a
plate of chop suey
in Ensenada
while a skeleton hand drew tiny x's
on a bottle of Carta Blanca

The all-night girls out on the Avenida

               what are they nymphs?

their painted lips & midnight eyes
accelerating the pulse of
glassy tides

Point Blank
Heavy action in & around the
revolving doors of perception

               Do I really need "permission"?

Subterfuge could be an escape
       perhaps by means of misdirection

The wind
             a breath of whispers
sublime & unreasonable
                  shredding the opulent
ocean air

Plug & Play
Something in immaculate day-glo
tips the rooftop shoving the rain
aside for a moment & setting the
moon down on the ground like a

machete on the red mud of the flood plain,
she said, & I said, yes,
certain emotions are like that

       & to defray the eternal
       verities no less
              like euphoria driven thru a
month of Sundays
     splashing shadows across the
                   Bhagavad Gita
in E-flat

There are other more expedient methods
I'm sure but
as for me I've always preferred the
scenic route

STALLING FOR DEPTH

It is Palm Sunday, a Tuesday, in September
& you're in La Jolla
a suburb of St. Paul, the Assassin

The fortune palms murmur
Sappho whispering to Homer
as an unspecified amount of rain falls
deflected by the windshield's
aura of confidence

The sky sort of breathing
a jungle of details
eucalyptic

couldn't tell if I was feeling exalted or exhausted
the giant agave overrun with
second & third thoughts

dancing in parentheses

Septremble, Octember, Nowonder

A single word read sideways could be your
ticket to "The Poems"

Satin & lace
Seaweed & foam

No one ever said it would be easy but it was
lessons I've learned at last
forgotten
where in other sentences if truth is beauty
it is again
but who will be there when the bell rings?

I don't know I'm asking

As I made my slightly unsteady morning rounds
I found a delicate, perfect spider web
shimmering in the sunlight,
so fine, precise,
like a transparent LP,
like the diaphanous skeleton of an LP,
suspended in the air above
the mint & ragweed

Chet Baker's solo on "Summertime"

(Yeah, fuck the liner notes, Jimmy)

Not to be otherwise
here where I am & you
are
drifting from one side of the beach to the other
one grain of sand at a time

SHOW ME THE WAY TO GO HOME

Had me a sky-gray Chevy once
w/a backstory that would've made
Coleridge weep

That was back when I used to listen to the
waves crash in the margins of
The Book of Songs
returning my dreams to their
default settings
always careful not to spook the horses

but no more than a tablespoon
as directed
& like Ali Baba bending over backwards
on Walking Crucifixion Day
I wore my hat execution style
because some things never change

THE SPANISH PRISONER

Heavy breathing & tattoo redundancy
occupy my narrow attention
as it were *The Day of the Locust*
between sips of swamp water
& the poems of Hart Crane
when a guy walks in w/a duck under his arm
(for medicinal purposes only)
like a trick you can do w/an
ordinary deck of cards
but dreaming it backwards
The Book of Waves
An Annotated List of Painkillers
Ecclesiastes (aka *The Guns of Navarone*)
& the winter sky
scarred like the underside of a skateboard
I mean you could
& tumble thru smoke rings
sampling the verisimilitude
burned into the lucid pavement
that still manages to rise up & catch
every step you take

Kevin Opstedal, 2025

Kevin Opstedal is the author of over 25 books of poetry including *California Redemption Value* (University of New Orleans Press, 2011) and *Pacific Standard Time: New & Selected Poems* (Ugly Duckling Presse, 2016). He is also the author of *Dreaming As One: Poetry, Poets, and Community in Bolinas, California, 1967-1980* (FMSBW: The Divers Collection, 2024). Along with having edited several little magazines, including *Gas: High-Octane Poetry*, he has published books by Joanne Kyger, Lewis MacAdams, Duncan McNaughton, and many others under his Blue Press imprint. Born and raised in Venice, CA, Opstedal currently lives in Santa Cruz.

THE PAGE POETS SERIES

Number 1
Between First & Second Sleep by Tamsin Spencer Smith

Number 2
The Michaux Notebook by Micah Ballard

Number 3
Sketch of the Artist by Patrick James Dunagan

Number 4
Different Darknesses by Jason Morris

Number 5
Suspension of Mirrors by Mary Julia Klimenko

Number 6
The Rise & Fall of Johnny Volume by Garrett Caples

Number 7
Used with Permission by Charlie Pendergast

Number 8
Deconfliction by Katharine Harer

Number 9
Unlikely Saviors by Stan Stone

Number 10
Beauty Will Be Convulsive by Matt Gonzalez

Number 11
Displacement Geology by Tamsin Spencer Smith

Number 12
The Public Sound by Marina Lazzara

Number 13
Record of Records by Rod Roland

Number 14
Strangers We Have Known by John Briscoe

Number 15
Cutting Teeth by Jesse Holwitz

Number 16
Other Scavengers by Lauren Caldwell

Number 17
Cueonia by Jesse Holwitz

Number 18
In the Museum of Hunting and Nature by Cynthia Randolph

Number 19
A New Species of Color by Tamsin Spencer Smith

Number 20
Busy Secret by Micah Ballard

Number 21
Out of the Blue by Fran Carbonaro

Number 22
Broadway Azaleas by Sunnylyn Thibodeaux

Number 23
War News II by Beau Beausoleil

Number 24
Hailstones by Justin Robinson

Number 25
Exile on Beach Street by Kevin Opstedal

www.ingramcontent.com/pod-product-compliance
Lightning Source LLC
Chambersburg PA
CBHW032037040426
42449CB00007B/926